ERICA T CAPRI

GEMLIGHT
PUBLISHING LLC

Southlake, Texas

Copyright © 2022 Erica T Capri

All rights reserved. No part of this publication may be reproduced, distributed, or transmitted in any form or by any means, including photocopying, recording, or other electronic or mechanical methods, without the prior written permission of the publisher, except in the case of brief quotations embodied in critical reviews and certain other noncommercial uses permitted by copyright law. For permission requests, write to the publisher, addressed "Attention: Permissions Coordinator," at the address below.

Gemlight Publishing LLC
2600 E Southlake Blvd, Southlake, Texas 76092

ISBN : 978-1-7367934-6-6

Gemlightpublishing.com

Ordering Information:
Quantity sales. Special discounts are available on quantity purchases by corporations, associations, and others. For details, contact the publisher at the address above.

Orders by U.S. trade bookstores and wholesalers. Please contact Gemlight: (833-436-5483)

Printed in the United States of America

Contents

Introduction 7

Self-criticism.. 16
Self-assurance...................................... 21
Self-defense 24
Self-narrative 28
Self-examination 32
Self-employment.................................. 35
Self-justification 39
Self-obsession 41
Self-determination 44
Self-appreciation 46

10-Day Self-Love Plan 48
About Erica T Capri............................ 61
Self-Love Promise Notes..................... 62

Introduction

Wow! I am so glad you acknowledge YOU NEED TO SHOW MORE SELF-LOVE!

Have you ever thought about a part of your created body that you like? What's the best part of you? A part that you adore? You have to be honest about it RIGHT?

Some of us frown at ourselves when we look in the mirror—our physical appearance is not the problem. You may have failed in relationships, jobs, perhaps in family issues. Whatever the case is, it causes the affliction of punishing yourself and not being true to yourself, not understanding your INNER BEING.

What is the INNER SELF?

Is it a person's internal mind, soul, or nature? The problem with society is that we have many people who are using external mindsets, causing them to be influential and in tune with internal mind control. The scariest part is that the external mindset of others is influencing that self-control and love, and this world is controlling your mind.

This leads to the whole dynamic of this book. It's a MIND GAME. Once the mind is right, and in control, the soul and everything else will fall into place.

I was one of the external mindset individuals. I was trapped in my own soul and had no escape plan. Are you in that maze of losing yourself and having no direction? Well, I am glad you found this book because I want you to find the love for your inner self.

Once you discover and realize the roots of how to escape, you will find yourself looking at life in a very different way.

Relationships will be better. Your love for others will be shifted to a higher level. WHY? Because when you love yourself, the love, joy, and happiness within will begin to glow through your veins and it will become NATURAL.

Are you ready to be FREE? To be filled with LOVE? Great, grab your favorite drink and come chill out with me for a while. LET'S TALK!!!

I am unapologetically in love with myself!

Self-love is a beautiful present that I give to myself each day.

If there is one thing that a human being can give to him or herself—it is to be genuinely in love with themself. God and the Universe created us to be who we are and to accept ourselves the *way* we are. We are not born in this world to become someone else. When we don't accept ourselves, we suffer. It's natural.

The very first thing that God gave us is the opportunity to be ourselves. Hence, it's essential to understand the value of self-love in life and change your life forever.

A few years ago, I remember that like every other person, I didn't know the real meaning of self-love either. I used to believe that self-love is selfish, and anyone who loves themselves acts out of their selfishness. However, I realized how wrong

I was and why self-love is a necessity as an internal process built over time.

I eventually discovered the beauty of self-love. I unlocked the secret of self-love and found that it's completely okay to love yourself unconditionally without explaining yourself. It's okay to be there for yourself when no one is. It's okay to stand for yourself and respect yourself enough to build boundaries around you.

Being faced with so many trials in life, God took me through a pruning season to learn to love *all* of me, the way he created me.

I decided to explore its true potential and find out how it really feels to be in self-love. My journey was filled with surprises. I didn't know one decision would change my life entirely! Initially, there wasn't much that I could understand about self-love. I knew that it was about loving yourself...but how?

How can I truly love myself, to be able to accept myself the way I am? I had lots of insecurities, fears, self-sabotaging thoughts, and self-judging behavior. Where there is self-love, there is no room for all these. How was I possibly supposed to get rid of them? Implementing such change in myself seemed like walking in a dark cave with no direction in sight.

But I had to, because there was one thing certain: if I wanted peace in life—I had to find a way. And that way is through self-love—the discovery of my inner me!

I remember seeing the movie "So Pretty" and the premise of that film was the main character had low self-esteem until she fell on her head, woke up, and then she had the most amazing self-confidence! It hit me that I wanted to have that confidence, love all my imperfections, the natural body God blessed me with—not worry about having the BBL or tummy tuck. I got exposed to the idea of self-love. Perhaps I was tired of judging myself for the trivial things that seemed important in my life? Or maybe because I was always finding myself struggling with having essential attributes, such as confidence, self-belief, trust, etc.

I always had trust issues with myself. I always put others first, neglecting my own happiness.

You don't really understand anything until you cross the threshold. I felt everything was normal with me. Having these thoughts were normal until one day, everything changed when I sacrificed my self-respect just to please someone else.

That day when I went back home, I cried a lot. I remember I cried until I could no longer see myself in the mirror. I was so ashamed of myself. I might not have got hit in the head like the lady in the movie, but pouring out my heart to love myself was the breaking point for me.

How could I disrespect myself and still be okay all these years? That thought alone shook me to the core. I remember that was the time when I disliked myself the most. I didn't want to do it. This moment taught me how torturing it is when you start disliking yourself and find it uncomfortable to stay with you.

This moment also taught me that if there is anyone who stays with you *all* the time, it is not any family member, partner, friend, or loved one—it is YOU. If you are not happy with yourself, you can never be happy with anyone else.

What is your life-changing moment for loving yourself? Have you experienced it yet? Maybe not, but that's what I want to help you develop—being in unconditional love with your inner self.

Self-love is like that. Self-love eliminated these doubts and freed me from the chains of self-sabotage. But how was I supposed to love myself when I had no idea where to start?

Some initial steps are shared below to help you master self-love. These steps helped me in my self-love discovery.

"What embitters the world is not excess of criticism, but absence of self-criticism."

~Gilbert K. Chesterton

Self-criticism

I was someone with low self-esteem. All through high school I had problems with my big nose, my chest was very small, I had a flat butt and was just skinny. I knew I had to eliminate self-made negative images, but how? One day I prepared myself a warm cup of coffee and sat down with my journal. I listed all the negative thoughts that I had for myself. Surprisingly, when I started writing—I realized that I had *too* many negative things to write about that I unknowingly believed, but they were not *true*. I was shocked to read how many lies I had been feeding myself for so long.

I took the journal with me and stood myself in front of the mirror. Then I repeated every sentence I wrote about myself while looking at my reflection. Clearly, after every sentence, there was a look of disappointment showing what I felt—I knew I was more than just the negative things I had written, but I had been feeling it all along. That hit me. That hit like a sledgehammer, like a slap on my face. I learned how ignorant I had been all this time.

This taught me that sometimes we are not really negative about ourselves, but make a judgment of ourselves based on society's expectations. The woman you admire has a banging body, or you were cheated on by your man, or maybe for men you want the six pack that the body builder has, or you have hair growth issues, or you gain weight, or didn't get the promotion on your job; your credit is bad—or whatever it is, society had you lock in on the mindset you are NOBODY!

I knew I wasn't most of what I wrote about myself, but I still took notice of what that irritating negative voice inside fed me. Taking it as a lesson, I deleted all that I wrote and turned them into positive affirmations. I wrote down the positive things that I truly felt about myself.

This small step entirely changed my life for the better.

Steps to do it:

1. It's okay if you are negative about yourself. Don't worry, it's perfectly normal. We are humans, and we tend to get negative. But dwelling on it for a long time is not normal. Noting down everything I felt helped me a lot in figuring out what I really was *not*.
2. Take an inventory of your strengths and write them down.
3. Once you do that, take them as an affirmation and record yourself

saying it, every morning when you get up or in your car, listen to your voice speaking the good within yourself.
4. Try to do something new or challenging either daily or weekly to help your mind stay away from the negative thoughts.

"Self-assurance doesn't come from looking perfect and having a great title, but from accepting yourself with all you mistakes and eccentricities."

~Cecelie Berry

Self-assurance

Once I figured out that I had these negative beliefs, I realized I needed to accept and not avoid them. The problem for the majority of us arises when we avoid accepting the truthful reality of our life. We start to feel socially avoidant and sometimes develop a pattern of isolating ourselves from social situations

Sometimes we know things we are not supposed to do, but we still do them. Accepting my own reality and taking responsibility for my emotions—both positive and negative—helped me accept myself.

There was no room for self-doubt and self-judgments when I started to accept myself the way I am. I assured myself that it's completely fine to have flaws and live contentedly with them. There is nothing wrong with accepting that you are full of flaws.

Steps to do it:

1. Actively praise yourself every day.
2. Stop comparing yourself to others; focus on your talents and do activities to enhance or grow to make you better than before.

"Respect your efforts, respect yourself. Self-respect leads to self-discipline. When you have both firmly under your belt, that's real power."

~Clint Eastwood

Self-defense

Self-love is a beautiful way of living life. When you are in love with yourself, you understand the habits that no longer serve you. There is a clear difference between what should be allowed and what not.

When I first learned the self-defense mechanism in self-love, I was told that it was selfish. But upon exploring it myself, I found how untrue that was. Protecting yourself from getting hurt, not allowing anyone to drain your energy, looking after your well-being, etc., can never be selfish. In fact, it is the most respectful thing you do for yourself out of pure love.

Loving yourself unconditionally gives you the freedom to filter out the kind of energy that may hurt you. It also allows you to welcome only those who genuinely love you and not the other way around. Surrounding yourself with the positive people who uplift you opens a new dimension of peace and happiness in life, which can be possible only because of self-love.

Remember, there is nothing wrong with protecting your sanity if you are in love with yourself. However, be honest about realistic goals so you won't risk disappointing yourself.

If you fail to do so it can cause you to disrespect yourself. You always want to be the first to respect yourself. Why? Because we would never allow anyone else to be disrespectful towards you. Self-love does the same for yourself. It never allows anyone to disrespect you.

Steps to do it:

1. Attract the right tribe. Reexamine your friends and colleagues that you surround yourself with.
2. Meditate on protection, refueling of the spirit.
3. Practice discernment.

> "Narrative thought is like leading someone to an invisible wall."

~Erica T Capri

Self-narrative

It is essential to observe the narrative inside our heads. That narrative lives with us all the time. Being mindful of it helps a lot in the journey of self-love. Now it's easier said than done. Listening to the voice is one thing but being cautious is another. Switching myself from being negative to positive took a lot of time, and, don't forget practice. It's not easy but not *hard* either.

Below are some of the steps that I used to convert the self-judgmental narrative into a positive one:

I knew I had low self-esteem hence low confidence. The negative voice inside my head always whispered ways of how others might judge me. It always stopped me from achieving possibilities in life. I remember even while talking, I lacked confidence and often stuttered while presenting my point of view in front of my colleagues or friends. I always had this fear that they might judge me, so I remained silent most of the time. This often drained my energy, eventually causing burnout.

Once I began to love myself, things started to change. I used the following affirmations that helped me a lot:

1. I am sexy/handsome the way I am. I don't need to adjust myself to others.
2. I love myself enough to live a happy life.
3. I don't need outside validation. I know I am enough for myself.
4. Others' points of view about me are not my responsibility. I

have nothing to do with anyone's opinion.

Once I switched my negative voice to the above affirmations, I noticed a drastic change in my lifestyle. Whenever I used to notice any negative thoughts about myself, I quickly recited one of the above self-made affirmations. It took me quite some time to reprogram my mind, but with practice, *I did it!*

"If you do not conquer self, you will be conquered by self."

—Napoleon Hill

Self-examination

- Am I good enough?
- Do I need to work out more?
- Am I smart enough to get that job?
- Will they accept me?
- What if they he/she don't find me attractive?
- Why will anyone want to hear my voice, speech, poetry or story?

These are some of the most common self-sabotaging thoughts that I used to have before I was introduced to the idea of self-love. I always found myself questioning my self-worth. At first, I felt there was nothing wrong with thinking about these questions. I felt this was part of life—but NO, it wasn't!

This way of thinking, in fact, sabotaged my self-image, causing distress, an invisible self-disliking, and negativity in me.

Unknowingly, when we have these thoughts, we are constantly sending signals to our subconscious mind that we are not worthy, we are not good enough, and nobody likes us.

Surprisingly, inside our head we are always listening to the voice that is talking, so it is essential to introspect on what we are speaking about.

Doing a routine self-examination of the internal language that I used helped me determine the root cause of my low self-esteem. It's like studying—understanding how you feel about yourself. It's a soothing experience to sit with yourself and talk about the emotions that are causing you delays and hindrances to moving on in your life.

"If you are going to achieve excellence in big things, you develop the habit in little matters. Excellence is not an exception, it is a prevailing attitude."

~Colin Powell

Self-employment

There is a reason why great scholars say follow your passion. Pursuing something you love is another form of self-love. Working hard to achieve your dreams as a side hustle or main job shows your love for yourself. It's respecting yourself enough to value the goals and responsibilities of yourself and others around you. I call it the **ultimate love.**

Earning my own living made me self-dependent, both financially and personally. Sooner or later, it made me realize my worth, enhancing my confidence as well. I led a happier life and added value to other people associated with me, either directly or indirectly. Making a direct source of income is giving yourself the opportunity to financially free yourself to do all the extra things you want to achieve.

Often, we hold to goals that we created ten years ago. We even go as far having the plan set in stone. But the spirit of fear keeps you entrapped to not step out in faith. You have to understand that if you have given any thought to making money or life improvements, or doing anything to help others—these are things that are your purpose and destiny for you to fulfill.

The most disappointing thing could be you sitting on a pot of GOLD and not wanting to share it with the world. You become stingy to something that you were chosen to fulfill while you are here on earth. What if it's taken and given to someone else? Guess what? It is and will be. Have you ever thought of something, an idea, business etc. and you find someone else has opened or performed that same project you were just thinking about? The problem is you have put it out in the universe, and now the thought has been processed and done—by the person with confidence to move forward *without any fear*.

"Obstacles don't have to stop you. If you run into a wall, don't turn around and give up. Figure out how to climb it, go through it, or work around it."

~Michael Jordan

Self-justification

There is no room to justify the negativity you have for yourself. I remember whenever I wanted to switch my thought process—my mind would always start justifying how wrong I was about it. The voice will always question being in love with yourself.

If I believed I was beautiful, the negative voice would always come up with excuses to trust the opposite. This is a big challenge that I felt while on my self-love journey. But every time my negativity began to take control over me—I quickly but gently reminded it that *it's not me*. My negative thoughts about me are *not me*.

"Know thy self, know thy enemy. A thousand battles, a thousand victories."

~Sun Tzu

Self-obsession

Self-love is all about accepting yourself the way you are—along with all the flaws you have. It is never about obsessing about being good and superior over others. The prevalent misconception about self-love is self-obsession. People often think obsessing about themselves is self-love. But it's not. Obsession, of any kind can never be healthy.

There is a difference between self-love and self-obsession. The problem arises when people take love as an obsession. Remember, self-love is healthy for you and every person around you, whereas self-obsession is unhealthy. It is not good either for your well-being nor for the people around you.

To understand what self-obsession is, notice how your behavior is with others. Notice how you talk to others. Do you always want to be the center of attention? Do you think you are better than others? If you have thoughts like this, please beware it's not self-love but self-obsession.

"The self is not something ready-made, but something in continuous formation through choice of action."

~John Dewey

Self-determination

While it may appear easy to say "I am going to love myself"—it actually wasn't. I had my share of ups and downs. Some days I would feel like going back to my old self and being done with all of this. But other times, I was determined to keep walking on this path and exploring self-love.

I am glad I chose the latter and continued doing it despite all the hardships I faced.

You have to be willing to set aside the pity party of feeling sorry for yourself and embrace the fact that you are GREATER!

"Love yourself enough to set boundaries. Your time and energy are precious. You get to choose how you use it. You teach people how to treat you by deciding what you will and won't accept."

— Ann Taylor

Self-appreciation

There is no other technique better than self-appreciation to be positive. Appreciating myself from time to time has helped me become who I am today. It uplifts my spirit to become a better version of myself.

Self-appreciation is like a catalyst for my personality development. It made me who I am today. No matter what kind of task I do, whether small or big---I always make sure to praise myself.

A little appreciation always makes things easier to keep going in the long run. It sends a signal to our subconscious mind that there is someone there that appreciates you. An appreciation from anyone always boosts our confidence, self-esteem, and self-belief.

When no one's praising you—why don't you do it yourself?

10-DAY SELF-LOVE PLAN

*H*ere's a quick 10 days that I planned to serve myself. This list helped me accept myself the way I am. Hope it helps you too.

Day 1: Reflect on yourself

Day 1 should be the "reflect on yourself" day. It was the day when I reflected on my strengths and weaknesses. I also made a list of the things I wanted to be and what my habits were—plus whether my habits are bad or good.

Day 2: Acceptance

On the second day, I decided to write down all my flaws. I was surprised at my flaws; it was like looking at a newer version of myself. The version that was always there, but I chose to ignore it. Accepting your flaws is a challenging task. It took me some time, but I started accepting my flaws one by one and gradually moved along with it.

Day 3: Time to pamper myself

The third day I dedicated to be there for myself. To do things I love to do. I picked my favorite activity—painting—and practiced it all day long. It made me feel good!

Day 4: Creating a journal

I sat down and created a journal. I wrote down all my feelings in it—emotions, sensations, impressions and everything in between.

Day 5: Finding out strengths

Now that I know what flaws I have, I planned to find out my strengths. I wrote down all the strengths I felt I had. Some of them were genuinely unique while others were not. This helped me boost my awareness of my strengths.

Day 6: Accepting my weakness

With strengths come weaknesses. Nobody is perfect; if you have strengths then you have weaknesses as well. Knowing your weaknesses helps you understand your potential. It also opens up doors to new challenges that you may be unaware of.

Day 7: Filling out the gaps

I call it the Ego Gap. We all have an ego, whether we accept it or not. The ego becomes a hindrance on the path of self-love. The gap between ego and unlocking your true potential by accepting your true self is what I call filling out the gap. Once this gap is filled, you can clearly see the horizon that awaits you.

Day 8: Meeting the new you

After following the 7 days challenge, the 8th day becomes the day when you meet a newer version of yourself. You will start noticing changes in you. These changes will unlock more potential.

Day 9: Confess the love

Today is the day I love myself while looking at my reflection. I confessed that I value myself, I love myself and I care about myself over all the negative voices I had for myself. It was effective.

Day 10: Self promises

Promising myself to love myself enough that I will always respect my boundaries. Self-promises show your self-value.

Hindrances in self-love
Self-love is filled with several challenges. Below are some of the most common challenges that you may face:

Learning to say NO: Remember saying no is absolutely normal and not disrespectful to anyone. In fact, it is respecting yourself.

Quit people-pleasing: People will never be completely happy with you no matter how hard you try. Pleasing people is disadvantageous to your mental health. Never indulge yourself in pleasing others.

Quit keeping yourself as your second priority: Make yourself the top priority. Learn to put yourself first before others. Normalize taking care of yourself first.

Stop always finding excuses to adjust: There is no need to adjust yourself in the world. Be natural and the way you are.

End the fight to fit in: You are naturally beautiful/ handsome the way you are. You don't need to fit in a world where you are not welcomed. By trying to fit in the world you indirectly lose your unique value.

About Erica T Capri

Erica T Capri is a compelling writer; with 15--years in literacy. She is the voice of Gem Talk Podcast and COO of Gemlight Publishing LLC. Her writing work has become popular with speaking engagements and film production. Erica happily resides in Dallas, Texas, and enjoys painting and spending time with her two teens.

Connect with the Author

SELF-LOVE *Promise Notes*

Date _____

I _____ Promise to

_____

_____

_____

_____

_____

_____

_____

_____

_____

_____

_____

Date _____

I _____ Promise to

_____
_____
_____
_____
_____
_____
_____
_____
_____
_____
_____
_____
_____
_____

Date _____

I _____ Promise to

_____
_____
_____
_____
_____
_____
_____
_____
_____
_____
_____
_____
_____

Date _____

I _____ Promise to

_____
_____
_____
_____
_____
_____
_____
_____
_____
_____
_____
_____

Date _____

I _____ Promise to

_____
_____
_____
_____
_____
_____
_____
_____
_____
_____
_____
_____
_____

Date _____

I _____ Promise to

_____

_____

_____

_____

_____

_____

_____

_____

_____

_____

_____

_____

Date _____

I _____ Promise to

_____

_____

_____

_____

_____

_____

_____

_____

_____

_____

_____

_____

_____

Date _____

I _____ Promise to

_____
_____
_____
_____
_____
_____
_____
_____
_____
_____
_____
_____
_____
_____

Date _____

I _____ Promise to

_____
_____
_____
_____
_____
_____
_____
_____
_____
_____
_____
_____
_____

Date _____

I _____ Promise to

_____
_____
_____
_____
_____
_____
_____
_____
_____
_____
_____
_____
_____

Connect with us
Facbook @ gemlightpub
Instagram @gemlightpublishing

To stay up to date about our books and authors.
Visit us at gemlightpublishing.com for our products and services.

www.ingramcontent.com/pod-product-compliance
Lightning Source LLC
Chambersburg PA
CBHW030044100526
44590CB00011B/327